T0151906

The Quality of Mercy

OTHER BOOKS BY PETER BROOK
PUBLISHED BY TCG

Evoking (and Forgetting) Shakespeare

The Shifting Point *Theatre, Film, Opera 1946-1987*

Conversations with Peter Brook *1970-2,000*
(Interviews with Margaret Croyden)

Peter Brook

The Quality of Mercy

Reflections on Shakespeare

THEATRE COMMUNICATIONS GROUP
NEW YORK
2014

Copyright © 2013, 2014 by Peter Brook

The Quality of Mercy is published by Theatre Communications Group, Inc., 520 8th Avenue, 24th floor, New York, NY 10018-4156

The essay entitled "The Quality of Mercy" was first published by the Temenos Academy, edited by Kathleen Raine. It has been revised for publication in this volume.

All Rights Reserved. Except for brief passages quoted in newspaper, magazine, radio or television reviews, no part of this book may be reproduced in any form or by any means, electronic or mechanical, including photocopying or recording, or by an information storage and retrieval system, without permission in writing from the publisher.

This volume is published in arrangement with Nick Hern Books Limited, The Glasshouse, 49a Goldhawk Road, London W12 8QP

This publication is made possible in part by the New York State Council on the Arts with the support of Governor Andrew Cuomo and the New York State Legislature.

TCG books are exclusively distributed to the book trade by Consortium Book Sales and Distribution.

A catalogue record for this book is available from the Library of Congress.

ISBN 978-1-55936-465-2 (paperback)

Front cover image © Shutterstock.com/Voronin76

Author photo by Régis d'Audeville

First TCG Edition, October 2014

For Nina

With a plea for mercy for all I've put her through with my countless illegible corrections, arrows, cuts and transpositions. I never would have believed that such patience was possible.

With love and gratitude,
Peter

Contents

Introduction   1

Alas, Poor Yorick   3
or What if Shakespeare Fell Off the Wall?

I Was There   19
How Mercutio Got His Laugh

Baked in That Pie   29
Cooking Up Titus Andronicus

Who Holds the Scales?   45
or Measure Still for Measure

Nor Live So Long   51
On King Lear

The Hour Glass   63
Every Grain Helps

A Cook and a Concept   75
  Dreaming the Dream

There Is a World Elsewhere   87
  The Readiness Is All

The Quality of Mercy   95
  On Prospero

Epilogue   109

A Chronology of Peter Brook's   111
  Shakespeare Productions

Index of Play Titles and Characters   115

Introduction

This is not a scholastic work. I try not to lecture on Shakespeare. This is a series of impressions, experiences and temporary conclusions.

The uniqueness of Shakespeare is that while each production is obliged to find its own shapes and forms, the written words do not belong to the past. They are sources that can create and inhabit ever new forms.

There is no limit to what we can find in Shakespeare. This is why I try to follow his example and avoid pedantry.

In Africa there is a saying: 'To be too serious is not very serious.'

Alas, Poor Yorick

or

What if Shakespeare Fell Off the Wall?

I was in Moscow giving a talk on Shakespeare for the Chekhov Festival. When I had finished a man got to his feet and, controlling his voice tense with anger, told the audience he was from one of the Islamic Republics in the South.

'In our language,' he said, '*Shake* means Sheikh and *Pir* means a Wise Man. For us there is no doubt—over the years we here have learned to read secret messages. This one is clear.'

So I was very surprised when no one pointed out that Chekhov must have been a Czech.

Since then, time and again, I have been told of still another claim to authorship of the Bard's works. The latest came from Sicily. A scholar had discovered that a family had fled from Palermo to England because of the Inquisition. Their name was Crollolancia. It is obvious: *crollo* means shake and a *lancia* is a spear. Once again the code is clear.

Some years ago, the most reputable of intellectual magazines asked a panel of scholars to explore the great question, 'Who wrote Shakespeare?' For some reason they approached me, and I wrote a very comic *reductio ad absurdum* of all the theories.

The editor sent it back with a cold note saying that, although they had commissioned my piece, it was not possible to publish it as it was not worthy of the high academic level they expected of their contributors.

What for them had been the last straw was my ending. I quoted a very distinguished English humorist from the beginning of the twentieth century, Max Beerbohm. His answer to the tortuous attempts to find hidden ciphers was to prove that the works of Tennyson had been written by Queen Victoria. To do so, he patiently scanned 'In Memoriam' line after line until he found one that he could reconstruct, using nothing but its letters. The result of his anagram was: 'Alf didn't write this I did Vic.'

We can all agree on one thing, at least. Shakespeare was and is unique. He towers above all other dramatists, the combination of genetic elements—or planets if you prefer—that presided over his appearance in the womb is so bewildering that they can only come together once in several millennia. It used to be said that if a million monkeys tapped on a million typewriters for a million years, the complete works of Shakespeare would appear. Even this is not sure.

Shakespeare touches on every facet of human existence. In each and all his plays the low—the filth, the stench, the misery of common existence—interweaves with the fine, the pure and the high. This shows itself in the characters he creates as much as in the words he writes. How could one brain encompass so vast a range? For a long time this question was enough to rule out a man of the people. Only someone of high birth and superior education could fit in the scale. The grammar-school lad from the country, even if gifted, could never leap over so many levels of experience.

This might make sense if his were not a brain in a million.

When we did research on the brain for a play, *The Man Who*, I met many phenomena. One aspect alone was the astonishing ability of many mnemonists. A typical case was a Liverpool taxi driver who had the entire layout of every Liverpool hotel room in his mind in vivid detail. So when he picked up clients at the airport he could advise them, 'No, Room 204 is not what you're looking for. The bed is too close to the window. Ask them to show you 319. Or even better, go to The Liverpool Arms and ask for Room 5—it's just what you need.' Such a prodigious memory did not come from higher education and in itself is not enough to write the works of Shakespeare. But he must have had an extraordinary capacity to receive and recall every sort of impression. A poet absorbs all he experiences, a poet of genius even more so; he filters it and has the unique capacity to relate apparently widely separate or contradictory impressions to one another.

Today, the word 'genius' is very rarely used. But all talk about Shakespeare must start from the recognition that this is a case of genius, and at once all the old-fashioned social snobbery is blown away. Genius can arise in the humblest backgrounds. If we look at the lives of the saints, unlike Cardinals and theologians, most were of very ordinary origins.

Jesus above all. No one doubts that Leonardo was truly Leonardo da Vinci, even though he was an illegitimate child from an Italian village. So why maintain that Shakespeare was a yokel? The level of education in Elizabethan times was remarkably high. There was a statutory principle that no country lad should be less qualified in classical knowledge than the sons of aristocracy. In the statute of the school in Stratford, it says: 'All sorts of children to be taught, be their parents never so poor and the boys never so inapt.' We can see the pleasure Shakespeare took in making fun of teachers. Classical information along with the pretentiousness of the pedants all entered into the vast storehouse of his brain.

Devoted and diligent scholars have done a stupendous task of investigation. Above all, James Shapiro has done magnificent work in bringing to life the taste and the throb of the time. He convinces through such detailed research that for once theories are replaced with vibrant experience. So we can imagine the young man from the country on his first days in London, walking the noisy, bustling streets, sitting in the taverns and peering into the brothels, his eyes and ears wide open, receiving impressions of travellers' tales, of rumours of palace intrigues, of religious quarrels, of elegant repartees and of violent obscenities. Given a unique avidity and power of receptivity, one single day—or, if you like, a week—could have given him more than enough material, social, political, intellectual, for a whole canon of plays. And in fact, year after year he lived with this ocean of information feeding the unformed stories swirling around in his head. It is not surprising that on the outside he was seen as a quiet man!

If a question of plagiarism were to arise amongst scholars, every don knows the hum of excited chatter that can delight the Senior Common Room. It is very strange that this has never led them to consider the most important vital factor in the Shakespeare story that his common room was the Theatre. Theatre is a community, and it is only within the life he lived day after day that all true investigation can start.

Who was this man, acting, rubbing shoulders in rehearsal, sitting for hours talking to all and sundry in the taverns without anyone suspecting he was a fake! An actor says to an author: 'Can't you change that line?' or 'This bit seems a bit long, couldn't we cut it?' or 'I haven't enough time for the costume change—could you write a soliloquy or a little scene on the forestage to help?'

Imagine a fake Shakespeare put on the spot. He has to rewrite and add a new scene. He ponders a while, works out how long it would take for a man on horseback to ride perhaps to Oxford or to York, wait for the secret writer to give him his papers and then to return. Shakespeare each time would have to hum and haw, then say, 'This will take me five days.' And nobody ever commented on this although it must have gone on year after year. No one smelt a rat amongst all those spiteful and jealous rivals? I'm sorry, academics—if you'd been part of any rehearsal process you would think differently. Even today, imagine a phoney writer. The cast would notice and gossip about the fact that every time you ask something, the author slips into the wings with his mobile phone.

As a manager, shrewd in business, Shakespeare often realised that his company could break up and salaries not be paid unless very rapidly he came up with a new hit. There is no document to show rewriting. In fact Ben Jonson underlines this. There were no plays waiting in drawers, unfinished, no writer's block— no Beckett-like perfectionism, rewriting draft after draft. His brain never stopped, searching and experimenting. He was like Mozart. If something of him was needed urgently, he at once drew on all the material vibrating inside him.

The theatre lives and breathes in the present, not in libraries or archives. In theatre today, yesterday, anywhere in the world, the author is present as a living human being. Shakespeare could not have arrived on the day of performance and, handing out to the actors the words they had to say, expect them a few hours later to perform *Hamlet* or *King Lear* with no preparation, no practising, no working out entrances and exits and the cues for music and the climbing from one stage level to another. Could this have been done with no questioning, no discussion, no trials and errors?

There were practical decisions to be taken. It is sufficient to look at Peter Quince in rehearsals with Bottom and the so-called 'mechanicals' in *A Midsummer Night's Dream*, or Hamlet's advice to the Players, to see concretely that, even if in Shakespeare's era productions did not have the complications of the present day, they still weren't haphazard happenings. They must have taken time, and there could not fail to have been questions, even disagreements, fired at the author—especially if he was also a member of the company well aware of the problems they had to resolve fast and together.

It is astonishing that in their search for evidence to support their theories, this fundamental aspect has been totally overlooked by so many scholars. Shakespeare was not a poet living on an island, he was writing for a community with a precarious way of life.

Apart from the actors, there were in the Globe, then as today, prompters and professional stage assistants doing the necessary functions under different names such as 'stage keepers'—who were omnipresent in rehearsal and performance to open and close traverse curtains, to stock and give out the props, to ensure the actors were on time for their entries and above all to keep order on stage and in the crowd—and in all the battle scenes, where there was an ever-changing number of crowd performers to be kept under control. These stage keepers were known sometimes to air loudly their judgement of a play—just like the gallants sitting on the Blackfriars stage making smart witticisms at the expense of the performers, as did the courtiers when watching *Pyramus and Thisbe*.

It is strange, even surreal, to imagine that Shakespeare working year after year with such weary and disgruntled employees, never had his qualifications put into question. All the theories that do not take into account rehearsals and performances float in thin air.

Of course, there are even today actors here and there who also have their pet theories. But they are few and far between.

Shakespeare's time was seething with dramatists good and bad, generous and spiteful. Most of them died poor, Shakespeare was one of the very few to retire with enough money to buy land. There was every reason for envy. Elizabethan London was no exception as everywhere writers always were trying to make a living, ready to issue pamphlets denouncing their fellows. Shakespeare was a perfect target. So is it not strange that there are no existing documents to denounce this fake actor-manager pretending to write and publish these very successful works under his own name? There is only the much-quoted snide words from Robert Greene, 'an upstart crow', balanced by the warm and even apologetic references by Ben Jonson praising a Shakespeare who for years had been his overt rival and yet one with whom he was seen spending hours together in the Mermaid Tavern. And how is it we can find no pamphlet on the comic rhyme that would have sold at every street corner with the same immediate success that all conspiracy theories and all exposures of secret lives have today?

In fiction there have been many cases of plagiarism and false identities, equally so in mathematics because there the work is done in isolation. But we must never lose touch with the communal nature of theatre. Theatre people often refer to themselves as a family. In a family all the secrets and lies are known to everyone.

There were the boy players—with the sharp insight and ready wickedness of all the kids in grown-up shows. Wouldn't they be the first to mock, to do irresistibly comic send-ups of the boss, ruling the show and pretending to be a poet? And could any of Shakespeare's fellow writers resist putting this into one of their own plays?

Jean Genet once said to me: 'Writers are very jealous creatures. If someone has a great success, it is a relief to hear that it was not he who wrote his work, but his cousin, and if this were really proved, then of course the envy would shift at once to the cousin.'

Neither Granville Barker, nor Henry Irving, nor John Gielgud, nor Laurence Olivier felt that the author they knew so intimately might be an imposter.

It appears that there are about seventy pretenders to the Shakespeare throne. There is even one woman, a Spanish/Jewish lady who is said to be the Dark Lady of the Sonnets. And there's a rumour that Queen Elizabeth wrote the plays in collaboration with an illegitimate son in an incestuous relationship! The defender of each of these pretenders works exactly like a criminal lawyer. He starts with the case he has to win, then, often very brilliantly, he brings all his erudition to convince the jury, outdoing in advance his opposing colleagues. And in most cases, we cannot fail for a moment to be convinced.

As far as I know, centuries went by before anyone questioned who the author was behind this name. Then one day, at the end of the nineteenth century, a lady in Boston who just happened to be called Delia Bacon woke up and decided that it must have been her great-great-great-grand-uncle who'd written the plays. And so the Impostor Industry started rolling. In hard times it's been a blessing—it's given mass employment: tenures to professors, advances to those who want to challenge the latest publication, and a boon to publishers with their attendant trades of printing, copy-editing, binding, distributing and bookselling. And of course critics now have a vested interest—like bankers—in keeping the ball rolling. If one of the first anti-Shakespeareans carried the god-given name of Thomas Looney, we can allow ourselves a smile.

Let's imagine the consequences today if Delia Bacon were to win. Irrefutable proof that Bacon had written every word. Then at once the birthplace would move to St Albans, and Stratford would crumble. And its three theatres and their bars and restaurants. And the Shakespeare Hotel and all the others. And the tourist buses and the gift shops.

In Stratford, the Town Council meets in panic and despair. Someone asks if it's not too late to have the writer of *Bacon, The Truth* eliminated? His house could catch fire and all the papers . . . 'What do you think, Chief Constable . . . ?'

In St Albans, the Town Council celebrates. Money is already rolling in. A fresh generation of actors, directors and architects discuss the new Festival Theatre. Flags, banners, T-shirts and pins are ordered. The Bacon Industry is under way and the scholar who has at last blown the whistle is knighted. Only the Marlowe Society is plunged into gloom.

There are many unanswered questions. Why didn't Shakespeare teach his daughter to read or write? Why did he not leave behind him any manuscripts? There certainly are gaps and holes in all we know about Shakespeare, but there are as many or more in each one of the other pretenders.

To sum it all up, there will always be a mystery. An enigma. Could there be a more fitting epitaph for the author of *Hamlet*? Certainly, every aspect of the story is full of unexplained contradictions. We can never know the answers. There will always be new claimants and new mysteries. In the end, simple common sense must prevail.

Everything we know suggests that Shakespeare was a very modest man. He does not use his characters to speak his thoughts, his ideas. He never imposes his world onto the world he lets appear. Ibsen did not hesitate to show what he felt about the society he lived in. Brecht wrote in order to demonstrate what was wrong in the world and how it should be changed. But again Shakespeare was unique. He never judged—he gave an endless multitude of points of view with their own fullness of life, leaving the questions open both to the humanity and to the intelligence of the spectator.

Shakespeare did not need ostentation. He did not try to assert himself and that is why there are none of the colourful anecdotes that biographers hunger for. Ben Jonson, with all his gift of caricature, could only find one adjective to conjure up this unassuming man—'gentle'. It is only in the privacy of the Sonnets that he speaks personally and even recognises the eternal value of the words that emerge from his pen. He was and is for all time completely self-effacing.

We can now conjure up the Gravedigger scene in *Hamlet*. Perhaps Shakespeare the actor is the gravedigger. At his feet, he sees his own skull. He takes it in his hand and for a long while peers wryly into the future. Then he murmurs softly, 'Alas, poor Yorick.'

I Was There

How Mercutio Got His Laugh

It was not easy to leave England just after the war, especially as one needed a special permit to carry the tiniest allowance of cash that even the simplest travel needed.

I had just done my first production, *Love's Labour's Lost* at Stratford, and was preparing to follow it with a *Romeo and Juliet* which I wanted to be young and full of fire. In those days, it was an accepted legend in the English theatre that only a mature actress in her forties could attempt to play Juliet. I hoped to smash this tradition by casting two very young actors as the star-crossed lovers. Above all, to get them to speak their lines with their own sense of truth. This meant being free from the established rules of verse-speaking.

My real interest was to discover the climate of the play, so my first trip was to Tangier to get a direct taste of the dust and blazing heat out of which fights and passions arise. This was an exciting revelation. The story did not belong to the polite world of Stratford and the genteel West End plays.

Next, another first. To Italy. This meant a beeline to Verona.

Despite the charm of any Italian small town, the comic side prevailed. Or perhaps it would be more accurate to say 'the commercial side'. As a child, I had been taken to Lourdes. This had left a distasteful memory of how the young Saint Bernadette was being exploited. In the narrow passage leading to the shrine, there were rows of shops each claiming to be more authentic than its neighbour and proclaiming 'Founded by the true family of Bernadette' or 'We are direct descendants of Bernadette'. In Verona, it was very similar. Every corner struggled to exploit Romeo and Juliet—'Here is the Capulet residence', 'This is where the Nurse went to market', 'Welcome to the fencing academy where the Montagues learned to use their swords', and 'Visit the exact spot where Mercutio died.'

One beautiful house had a sign saying 'Birthplace of Juliet'. I went in. It was lunchtime. I was alone, but for a very distinguished elderly Italian who was my guide. His speech was beautifully delivered as he followed me from room to room. Juliet's bed, the closet where the Nurse slept, the balcony—the famous balcony itself with a splendid view across the beautiful Veneto landscape—the parents' wing where the family dined. And then down a narrow stone stair into the cellar. Here my guide pointed to a large stone slab! 'This is where they brought Juliet's corpse; it was through this narrow opening that Romeo came—you can imagine the painful sight that confronted him—his lifeless bride. He clasped her in his arms.' The guide leaned respectfully across the cold slab. 'We have here a dagger—the actual one—and, after kissing her—' the guide mimed the action—'and taking the poison from her lips, Romeo took his own life.'

It was a fine performance, one he clearly repeated day after day. He then led me up the stairs to the front door. I was so struck by his well-schooled intelligence that I could not restrain myself. 'Tell me,' I asked, 'you are such an educated person. How can you bear day after day to tell these tales as though you believe them—when you know they haven't the least root in truth? In England,' I said, 'we all know there were no such persons as Romeo and Juliet.'

He paused. Then with exquisite courtesy he replied, 'Yes, indeed, it's true. And here in Verona we all know there was no such person as Shakespeare.'

We parted amicably, and as I plunged into the bustling streets, they seemed more crowded than ever. A poster caught my eye and gave me the answer. That evening in the open-air amphitheatre there was to be the very first performance in Verona of *Romeo and Juliet*. The city had lived, grown, vastly profited from a play no one had ever seen. It would be an extraordinary event. I could hardly believe my luck. I had to be there. So I joined an endless queue, buzzing with anticipation as it edged forward. I got one of the last tickets and found myself in a vast amphitheatre facing the longest stage I had ever seen. A grand spectacle.

In England, we were just beginning to revolt against the nineteenth-century belief that poetry was a language of charm and prettiness, to be half-sung in Pre-Raphaelite scenery. In this world of souvenir shops and trinkets I knew in advance what the audience would expect. *Romeo and Juliet* would be a delightful story, like Rossini without the music, to which nice families could take the children.

The orchestra tuned up. A little overture, and the play began. Conventional Italian actors entered in period costumes, trained in the old-fashioned Stratford manner of the time. Everyone in the audience seemed delighted. I had been wondering how the racy humour that runs through all Shakespeare's plays would go down with this audience. I was sure 'the bawdy hand of the clock is on the prick of noon' would not be understood by the Italian translator, and in its place, a line that could be spoken in the best society. But I had not reckoned on the moment when Mercutio says to Romeo: 'O that she was an open-arse and you a poperin pear.' This was faithfully translated. There was a gasp. Over a thousand people held their breath. Could they have this time heard rightly? Could this lewd humour have come from the pen of the great Romantic poet? First reaction—this could not be authentic, not Verona's Shakespeare. Then suddenly an explosion of laughter, the richest belly laughs I have ever known. So Shakespeare was a real human being. The poet's pedestal swept away. Everyone relaxed, ready to savour each twist of the play in a completely new way.

Shakespeare's legend had made the city prosperous but the real man now belonged to the city.

I returned to England. The journeys were over, and the practical work on *Romeo and Juliet* began. I had two marvellous collaborators: Rolf Gérard, who would become my close friend and designer over many years; and an outstanding Catalan-Swiss composer, Roberto Gerhard, who had just made a striking debut with a score for a radio version of *Don Quixote*. Both at once felt the heat and passion of the play. The set that gradually arose was little more than a blazing orange stage cloth, like a bullring.

Together, with a very dynamic instructor, we plunged into rehearsal with our young cast, who were delighted to begin the day with dangerous rapier fights. We made many mistakes and learned many lessons, but when the first night came, the play unfolded to the Stratford audience on the hot orange stage. The audience, unlike the one in Verona, were dismayed and taken aback. I was attacked for ruining the poetry and wasn't invited back for many years.

A few days after the opening, the theatre had arranged a public question-and-answer session. When I arrived backstage, I was met by an anxious stage manager. 'I must warn you,' he said. 'You're in trouble. Prepare for the worst.' I stepped into the arena. The good and loyal Stratford audience was there. A long silence was broken by a lady rising to her feet, clearly trembling with indignation.

'I would like Mr Brook to explain to us why, at the opening night of *Romeo and Juliet* in the Memorial Theatre, there was no light—in the ladies' cloakroom!'

This got a laugh, but the discussion was heated. And inevitably the press was damning. However, I was already beginning to discover that while praise is for a moment reassuring, the valuable criticisms are the ones that are clearly from an unbiased and intelligent mind. They make one think.

Despite the inevitable disappointment, gradually I saw all that *Romeo* lacked. There was plenty of fire, colour and energy—which brought us a small minority of enthusiasts. But what was missing was an overall tempo, an irresistible pulse to lead from one scene to another. I had not yet learned that this was the basis of all Elizabethan theatre, and so began a long period of discovery. The theatre of the day, based on well-made West End plays, with their two intervals, had long lost all contact with the relentless Elizabethan rhythm. Each scene had to lead to another, never letting the audience go. Each scene had to be a stepping-stone for the next—there were no curtain breaks and pauses; no new scenery to get accustomed to. And not only did this demand a constant moving forward, it also made contrasts, unexpected changes of rhythm, tones, levels of intensity. In this *Romeo* I had worked scene by scene, each with its beginning, middle and end.

The big revelation came later when working in opera. In music, I saw that a series of notes is a world of infinitely tiny details which only exist because they are part of a phrase. A phrase in turn is inseparable from a driving forwards. Just as in a speech, a phrase is a thought that prepares and leads on to the next one. Only an insufferable bore goes on repeating a phrase long after we have got its meaning. A play of Shakespeare's must be played as one great sinuous phrase, never ending before the very end.

When after two years of opera I returned to Stratford to direct *Measure for Measure*, I found that the immersion in music had brought me a new awareness of tempo and phrasing.

There's an old cliché that Shakespeare could easily have written film scripts. Indeed, when a film is placed in the projector—to use the out-of-date jargon of the day—and the spools begin to turn, there is a movement, and with it the interest of the viewer is held. This has to be maintained till the end of the last shot. It applies to every category: art film, thriller, Western. They all were called 'movies'. This led to the need to be free of the locked-in nature of the scenery that seemed so necessary at the time.

I was only asked back to Stratford when the direction changed many seasons later. This exile was clearly a stroke of fortune, as my approach had been transformed by so many experiences.

Baked in That Pie

Cooking Up *Titus Andronicus*

When cubism was first greeted with howls of incomprehension, Gertrude Stein saw this as a clear example of how each century continues to see the present through the eyes of the past. Today, we can begin to recognise how previous centuries have influenced our attitudes to Shakespeare.

When I first worked at Stratford, there was the same handful of plays that were repeated each season. The others were less popular as they were considered of minor interest.

The middle-class spectators were still Victorians and quite naturally viewed the plays in the way Romantic painters had shown them. My first production, *Love's Labour's Lost*, was also influenced by the post-war reaction against four years of drabness and austerity. We longed for elegance and charm. I could not find them in the inevitable Elizabethan clothes, which for me were drab and conventional. So I found what T. S. Eliot called 'the objective correlative' in my newly discovered love for the eighteenth-century French painter Watteau. I imposed him on a reluctant designer, and certainly the stage picture had a freshness and charm that in no way violated what audiences expected of a comedy of lightness and grace. But what intrigued me in Watteau was that apart from the elegant gallants, the lute players and the slightly melancholic harlequins, there was always a mysterious figure on one side, silently watching the revels. This was both an enigma and a clue. One day, its message became clear. At the end of *Love's Labour's Lost*, the joyful party is suddenly interrupted by a messenger carrying to the Princess news of her father's death. In every production of the day, this was taken as a convenient way of bringing the play to an end. But this seemed to overlook the intuition of the young Shakespeare that lightness needs the shadow of darkness to make it real. So, when at last all misunderstandings in the story seem joyfully to come to an end, a sombre figure would appear on the skyline. At once the revels are over, the Princess and her court have to leave with no possibility to resume the budding love affairs until after a year of mourning. The last songs are tinged with melancholy, they express summer giving way to winter, and the play ends in suspension, with a haunting line: 'You that way, we this way.' Already we can sense a hint of a *Twelfth Night* to come. From this, we can follow a straight line to the moment when, in *Measure for Measure*, Isabella has every reason to take revenge on her brother's apparent murderer. The sordid city where the action takes place seems to suggest no pity. She searches deeply into the darkness of her heart. In a way that seems to foreshadow Dostoyevsky, she falls on her knees to beg for mercy. At once, the play is flooded with light.

When I worked on *The Winter's Tale*, the same quality gradually appeared in a different sequence. The play is clearly divided into three parts. First, a sombre melodrama that is almost a tragedy. Then, suddenly comes the switch to the radiant innocence of a pastoral. And just as unexpectedly to a third part, to the desolation and ashen penitence of Leontes, doomed to live with the statue of his dead wife as a constant reminder of his folly. Crime, yes, and punishment, but clearly Shakespeare could not stop here. Leontes sees his long-lost daughter entering his palace side by side with his enemy's son. Uncannily, they so resemble his dead wife and her suspected lover. For a moment, time stops. Leontes is given another chance. He takes it, and, in Shakespeare's most astonishing and deeply moving stage invention, the statue returns to life, and the end radiates forgiveness and love.

Another neglected work, *Timon of Athens*, was conveniently written off at the time as a first sketch, a poor man's *King Lear*. So, Timon was seen as a sweet old fuddy-duddy, put in the doghouse, not yet by his daughters but by his greedy creditors. It's not surprising that the play rarely appeared, having so little to attract actors, directors or audiences.

One day, I saw a production that changed everything. It was played by Paul Scofield, who showed us Timon as a successful young man at the top of his career. Years later, when looking for a Shakespeare play to open our newly found Bouffes du Nord in Paris—and *Romeo and Juliet* had been suggested as the obvious choice—this Timon came to mind. In our first International Centre group that had just completed its African journey, there was a brilliant young actor, witty, attractive and dynamic—François Marthouret. With him, the play took on an immediacy for the Paris audience. It had a freshness and an impact that none of the familiar old favourites could have brought. Nineteenth-century attitudes to business and success were being questioned. The lure of fortune, the roulette of partners and associates, the lightness of friendship became immediate and real. There was no need for mobile phones or dark ties. This was exactly why Jan Kott had named his book *Shakespeare Our Contemporary*. The play was for now.

But the Victorian attitude was more deeply entrenched than anyone imagined. There were moral limits, and one play was beyond the pale: *Titus Andronicus*.

There was no way out. If this was truly the Bard, the only service to be rendered was to make sure that such an indecent collection of horrors was never to be seen by the public, especially in the place of his birth.

Titus had been lurking in my subconscious since student days. As the art world was becoming more and more aware of the force and beauty of what was given the condescending label of 'primitive' art, the more the barbaric nature of Roman ferocity took on a splendour. Wasn't there, I asked myself, lurking under the typically Elizabethan horror play, something that came from deep down in Shakespeare's as yet unexplored subconscious? Wasn't he, like Picasso and the much-admired British sculptor, Jacob Epstein, having his imagination fed by archaic images buried deep in ancient limbos? In Norman England, Saxon roots were never completely forgotten. The Roman relish for blood sports, gladiators, fights with lions, could not destroy their true Greek-tragedy heritage—Electra, Medea and the terrible acts of catharsis which sublimated the horror. I felt that *Titus* could take on a new power if it could discover an underlying ritual with the ferocity present in Icelandic and Saxon mythology. In fact, we can even see almost identical elements in Aztec cultures. Under a pitiless sun, still-beating hearts were ripped out with obsidian knives. If we could link back to their tradition, a new barbaric splendour could emerge that would give the *Titus* a savage nobility.

Clearly, the play was waiting patiently for the time it could emerge from oblivion. When the moment was ripe, all the necessary elements came together.

Glen Byam Shaw, director of the RSC, was building a season around Laurence Olivier and Vivien Leigh. So he had no difficulty in assembling a company of the best English actors of the day. He asked me if I would be interested in directing a play: 'How about *Titus*?' My reaction was an immediate 'Yes!'

I had been on bad terms with Olivier since our feuds during the filming of *The Beggar's Opera*, but his clever wife, Vivien Leigh, drew us together again. One of Olivier's great qualities was to bring a very detailed reality to characters who could too easily become stereotypes or abstractions. He had triumphantly used his charisma and sexuality to turn *Richard III* from a vehicle for ham acting into an irresistibly seductive, brilliantly intelligent and thus dangerous despot. In the same way, he had given an unforgettable presence to normally small roles— Justice Shallow in *Henry IV* and the Button Moulder in *Peer Gynt*. He began every new part with experiments to give himself a new voice—and often a new nose. He plunged into the apparently conventional role of Titus the avenger and at once uncovered a real man. Above all, it was Vivien Leigh who brought a quality no one could ever have associated with Lavinia, finding a beauty and a poetry in her misfortune. So Lavinia, raped and with her hands cut off—which we suggested just with a red ribbon falling from her fingers to the ground— turned this nasty piece of Grand Guignol into a haunting moment of beauty. It was as though Vivien's grace and talent could transform this play, in the way that the Japanese theatre transforms awesome acts of cruelty in Kabuki legends.

For the other parts, there were the remarkable actors that Glen Byam Shaw had assembled. Aaron was not just a black villain, a stock figure already much used in Elizabethan plays. Of course, in those days the possibility of having a black actor to play a black character did not even occur to anyone. One black American, Paul Robeson, had played Othello and that was about all. Africans and black Americans were only considered useful for jazz, singing and dancing. Anthony Quayle approached the part with respect and humanity. The tenderness of his relationship to his black baby was unforgettable. In the same way, Maxine Audley found unsuspected depths in the ferocious Queen of the Goths.

At the time, a play could not exist for me without pictures. It seemed vital to develop a stage metaphor that from the start could open us to an unknown world. I had already had the rewarding experience of working with very talented and imaginative designers. And I had also made the discovery that the evolution of patterns of staging, which for me was a long process of trial and error, was often blocked by the speed with which many designers found their solutions. These were at once crystallised into images. Worst of all, they seemed totally convincing. Then, later in the process came the moment when they no longer were in harmony with the new forms arising in rehearsal through the work of the actors. The breakthrough came at Stratford when I found a new way of work which lasted for many years. The Head of Construction and the Head of Costume were two very sensitive and capable men. I found I could work directly with them. For *Titus*, large columns of black and gold were built with simple but amazing mechanisms that the scene-builder was thrilled to invent. They opened up on different levels to reveal blood-red chambers or twisted forestry. By the carpenter's ingenuity, the fluting of classic columns could swing out, suggesting sombre trees.

Sound had to be an inseparable part of what the imagery was evoking. This was when tonal and atonal music was giving way to what preceded electronics— it was called 'concrete music' and I visited its pioneer, Pierre Henry, in his Paris studio. The techniques were very accessible. They involved recording a slab of sound and then carving from it what one wished by changing its speed and pitch, mixing and combining more and more tracks, then cooking the rest as one pleased. I made experiments, putting a very ordinary microphone inside our piano, tapping the chords on the iron frame and using the pedal as a percussion instrument, so that all the overtones of the piano were awakened. When a simple rhythm was added, this gave us a march from ancient times and provided Olivier with a deeply impressive first entrance. No one noticed that the three notes extracted for the overtones were in fact 'Three Blind Mice'.

For Olivier, a new role was always special, and he confided to me his secret ambition. It was in the last scene when Titus had taken his revenge for the rape of Lavinia by chopping the sons of the Queen of the Goths into small pieces and baking them in a pie. The climax of the play is when the Queen asks where her sons are, and Titus answers, 'There . . . in that pie.' Perhaps of all the pieces of crude melodrama this was what for so long made the play seem too preposterous to stage.

Olivier took this as his greatest challenge. He knew that the first-night audience in Stratford was there to laugh at a ridiculous play brought out of the cupboard. This would be the ultimate moment of mockery. By the intensity of his concentration, the tension of his speaking, he succeeded at the premiere. He set out to turn this into a chilling moment of truth. Then, relishing the danger and the call of the impossible, he repeated this with every audience in each country where we played. Because there was a long continental tour.

It began in Paris where the Oliviers were the toast of the town. But as it moved across Europe to Belgrade and Venice, a true tragedy began to emerge behind the lurid events of the story. Vivien Leigh's mental health steadily deteriorated. It had begun when she had seen herself in Elia Kazan's film of *A Streetcar Named Desire*. Karl Malden grabbed her by the neck, thrust her in front of a mirror and held a naked light bulb onto her face. She was known as one of the world's most beautiful women. The shock of seeing herself and her real age so pitilessly revealed was more than she could take. The tremors remained hidden through rehearsals and the excitement of the opening. She knew that it was her grace and beauty that were an essential element in the audience's discovery of the play.

Yet, as the tour continued, a daily roller-coaster of mania and depression took over. She would rush to all the antique shops and, to the despair of Larry, larger and larger boxes, and even crates, accumulated in their hotel rooms. When we arrived in Vienna, despairingly he turned to me for help. So I spoke firmly to Vivien: 'You must see a doctor.' To my surprise, she took this very calmly. 'I've been refusing this,' she said. 'But now it is different. I have a very old friend who works here. He is a doctor. If you can find him, I promise I'll listen to anything he has to say.'

It was not so easy. There was no trace of anyone with his name in the Vienna phone book. In the directory, people were listed with their professions. In the end, we found someone in an outer suburb. He was described as a writer and translator. I showed this dubiously to Vivien. 'Yes! That's him,' she cried. 'It doesn't say he's a doctor,' I ventured. She giggled delightedly. 'I've got you! . . . You said "doctor". You didn't say what doctor. You said you wanted me to see a doctor. He's a doctor. A Doctor of Philosophy. I'd love to see him again!' And she choked herself with laughter.

After this, the tensions of daily life matched and outdid those of the play. In Yugoslavia, we were given a burly guide called Boris whose job was to accompany us everywhere. Vivien at once adopted him as her servant and would disappear with him at the end of the performance. She insisted on being taken to a hideout on the main motorway and had spent all night drinking and revelling with the truck drivers. When the bill was brought, she would wave her hand: 'Boris! You pay!' He took this in his stride. Clearly, the secret police could afford it.

But her performance began to suffer. We went on to Warsaw where there were correspondents for English newspapers, and our daily task was to see that no rumours could emerge in the press. But when we landed at London, there had to be an ambulance waiting for her at the airport. The tour had just made it without a scandal.

In England, France, Italy, the play was welcomed and appreciated as a beautiful theatre experience. At no point did it strike the often sophisticated spectators that it could also be real. In Belgrade, the horrors were part of daily life. Just before we arrived, a man being interrogated by the police had been thrown out of their sixth-floor office window. In a lightning reflex, he caught hold of the ledge. One of the police drew out a knife and cut off his hands. He fell, screaming, to his death.

Nowadays, this is commonplace. It is reflected in plays and films. But unlike Shakespeare, we have become incapable of recognising, at the very same moment, another reality—the richness and magic of life. Vivien could sense this. As she held up her mutilated stumps, the gasp of the audience went beyond horror.

Since we are no longer comfortable Victorians, *Titus* today has found a normal place in the Shakespearean canon. It is like so many contemporary plays and films. But with a difference. The young author who was also using the popular, violent themes of his time. But he was already Shakespeare, a poet; he could not fail to go beyond and behind the surface, to a sense of such horror that it creates awe.

A Hollywood producer, Sam Spiegel, had been very moved by the performance. He offered me the possibility of filming it in ten days as a direct recording. This excited me, as I saw within his budget the possibility to use the widescreen Cinemascope that was just coming into fashion to make a version that instead of copying the stage would be like an epic fresco. There was a completely unexpected obstacle. Olivier refused. He explained that his next project was to direct a film of *Macbeth* with himself in the title role and with Vivien as his lady. He wanted to do this as a real film with a long shooting time and a heavy budget. He had already done this successfully with *Richard III* and *Hamlet*. 'If you show it's possible to make a Shakespeare film in three weeks and cheaply, I won't have a chance!' Once again, our relationship soured, and after the *Titus* project was abandoned, the curse of the Scottish play worked on Olivier. Despite being at the height of his career as a star, both in movies as in the theatre, Olivier just could not find the backing he needed. His project, too, fell by the way.

Today, I feel that our *Titus* belonged to its time and must only remain a memory. The play must be brought to life again with the eyes of today. With the eyes of the past, refreshed by a sense of the reality of the present, the plays show us new shapes, new mountains and chasms, new lights and new shadows. We are amazed that we had not been aware of them before.

Shakespeare's plays are like planets which in their endless movement, for a moment, come closer to us, then whirl back into orbit.

Who Holds the Scales?

or

Measure Still for Measure

In *Measure for Measure*, Shakespeare typically makes links between sky above and mud below. He refuses the customary dichotomy. Excrement has its place; it fertilises the soil and surprising plants can grow. And rain comes down from the sky. In the play, there are two worlds: the refined world of the palace and the squalor of the brothels, the prisons and the street. The trigger of the whole action is the Duke's intuition that he has no real awareness of life, no true understanding, and so is incapable of fulfilling the role of a Duke. But what is order, what is authority without injustice? The play gives immediate life to these eternal questions. The Duke, whose name, Vincentio, like Angelo, contains a medieval reference to the divine, unwittingly sets in motion a mechanism in which he, Isabella and Angelo have to confront and unravel their own deepest contradictions. In my first production at Stratford after *Romeo* had sent me into exile, the first step was visual. How to find a world in which this story could unfold convincingly? It was in Brueghel and Bosch that the keys seemed to lie.

In Bosch, there is the ultimate relishing of crudeness, dirt, vulgarity—in Brueghel, the tension and the pain of the Middle Ages is tempered by eyes straining for hope and meaning. Without being literal, we found out simple architectural forms that could set the Duke and the prisoners in the same world. The aim was to keep the action fluid, with no breaks between scenes, only images that could dissolve from place to place without breaking the continuity. Above all, in Stratford, I was working for the first time with John Gielgud. He bravely played his first middle-aged part without a wig, just with his own balding head. And a fine actor, Harry Andrews, as the Duke disguised as a monk, was a white-robed figure crossing the darkness.

The key to the story is Isabella. The first scene—when we see her in a convent as a young votary—cannot be ignored. She has taken a vow, a vow to Heaven, with all her integrity and belief. This makes a loss of chastity unthinkable. Many years later at the Théâtre des Bouffes du Nord we did a workshop on *Measure* with young people from the roughest of Paris's outer suburbs, all Muslim. I told them the story, and they improvised it as we went, scene by scene. When it came to the scene between Isabella and her brother Claudio, sentenced to death for adultery, everyone could share both sides of the painful clash between family love and religious laws. Isabella would give everything for her adored brother—except her chastity. For many English actresses this needs many psychological twists and hang-ups to make it real. For an Islamic audience it was obvious. But when her brother, Claudio, could not accept this—when the price was his own life—again everyone felt for him as well. Then suddenly in pure improvisation, the actor playing Claudio broke down and cried out, 'If I had to be buggered by fifty men to save your life, do you think I would hesitate?' A gasp was followed by a long silence. This group no longer needed to have explained to it what theatre is.

Measure for Measure lives up to its title—its rich variety of elements needing constantly to be held in balance. Every character, every incident has its place, as our sympathy and understanding swing from one to the other. To respect and renew this balance is every new production's task. We must be led step by step to an impasse, where there seems to be no honourable way out. Then Isabella's astonishing call for mercy, harmonising with the Duke's own process of self-discovery, tips the scales again, and for a moment they become level.

If it is a great mistake to try psychologically to explain away Isabella's vow of chastity, in the same way it is a crude modernism to make the Duke into an unscrupulous manipulator. It may be hard for us today to accept purity of intentions, but this is fundamental to Shakespeare's explorations of what can surpass conflict and contradiction. This is an often neglected key to Othello's murderous rage. For Othello, a woman is a symbol of purity—virgin. Purity belongs to God and a betrayal of purity is far more than the betrayal of a wife. It is defiling the sacrament; a chaste woman's pure nature expresses itself in outer form. As in *Antony and Cleopatra*, *Othello* is a clash between Eastern and Western ideals.

In one of the early scenes, Desdemona is surrounded by friends chatting and laughing with a social charm and delight that is typically Western. For us, this is natural and engaging. But to a Moorish observer, it expresses a woman contaminated by degraded values. The ground for an Iago is well prepared. If this theme fascinated Shakespeare, it is not surprising that he returned to it in *Antony and Cleopatra*. While Othello is a man at the summit of his military career, with the strength to kill and be killed, Antony is on Sunset Boulevard, his star is falling, and in the brilliant Egyptian he finds again his youth and temperament. In *Measure*, the Duke is stronger than Angelo; there is no real struggle between them. We can see the thread that leads through so many good and bad Dukes to Prospero. But on the way, we find the only case where all these human facets of strength and weakness are in one character—Lear.

Nor Live So Long

On *King Lear*

The name 'King' means 'He who has the last word', the absolute despot. It is intoxicating to have such power but it can create deep and unknown problems. In ancient times, so the story goes, an ageing King would sit every night in his garden, knowing that sooner or later a young man would penetrate all the defences and climb over the wall. The King constantly prepares himself for the final combat. If he is killed, the stranger becomes the new ruler.

In our times, we have seen how painful it is for a dictator to accept that the end must come. A long series of leaders have had terminal illnesses that came from stress—how much from the daily strains of office, how much from watching the wall for the stranger to appear. When they learn that they have an incurable malady, they begin searching first in books and then amongst the vast circles of presidential advisers to discover the meaning of this inacceptable phenomenon they could not dominate—death.

As the old proverb says, 'Pride goes before a fall.' Lear at the start has every reason to be proud: he is on top of his ladder, on top of his form. It is a very sad error for players and directors to show Lear in the first scene as a feeble old man already in his dotage. Even Laurence Olivier was caught in this trap—in his own words: 'To give away his kingdom he must have been a silly old fart!' As a result, the first appearance of his Lear was high comedy—his guards stood to attention while the King, passing through them to his throne, paused to poke some of them in the ribs, with a chuckle. Of course, he got his unexpected laughs, but the price was high. There was nowhere for the character to go for the rest of a long play, there was no tragedy and it was only the superb Fool of Alec Guinness that saved the day. Guinness had an expressionless snow-white face, an actor's mask. When he just sat, said, 'I'll go to bed at noon,' and died, we saw there was nothing at all within, just an empty eggshell. This alone was worth the trip.

In fact, we need only to listen to Lear's first lines to see that he was fully on the ball. His decision to divide his kingdom was the practical reflection of a hard-bitten man-of-the-world. He recognises that the time for him has come, and he announces that his primary motive is 'that future strife may be prevented now'. This is the testament of a shrewd ruler. He knows only too well the ambition and factions simmering under the surface in his court, waiting for him to die. Also, with equal shrewdness, he realises that a division into two is always the basis for conflict. A division into three contains a natural balance of forces.

How often have Goneril and Regan been reduced to comic-strip caricatures, as two slinking, evil sisters? Are we sure that they are not proud of their father on this great day? When called upon to declare in public their devotion, is it all scheming hypocrisy? Is there not a reflection of what every loyal courtier constantly tries to express in well-educated elegant terms? When Prime Ministers go to visit the Queen, do they not leave their homes with prepared words of homage which, at the moment, are sincerely meant?

The first shock for Lear is when he is denied what he believes to be his due—total gratitude from all his subjects and most of all, from his children. Until he goes out into the storm, his defences are intact. They show his absolute need to reaffirm his commanding presence. He is a man of power which he can use, manipulate or disguise when it suits his purpose. But here he is caught by surprise, and the volcano under the surface is suddenly out of control. How could his favourite daughter so wantonly destroy a great public occasion?

Then Lear's surprise and his rage take on a terrible inevitability. In the same way, Shakespeare avoids simplifying the character of Cordelia, for her reaction is equally inevitable. She has the uncompromising strength of her father in her blood.

The second appearance of Lear shows us the other side of the coin, how the cauldron of his energy made the King such a splendid companion for his knights. He has the traits we find in so many dictators—Stalin was Papa Stalin to so many; all the worst monsters of our time seemed amiable, generous and very good company, especially to foreign visitors. When Marshal Tito came to our *Titus Andronicus* in Belgrade, he did not wear his customary uniform. In a dark suit, black tie and white shirt, he could easily have been mistaken for a successful Hollywood producer as he poured out drinks for the cast in the interval. Even Hitler charmed many of the ruling classes, not only in Britain, as did later Saddam Hussein and Colonel Gaddafi.

Their last days and their way of death uncovered the horrific scale of their inner violence and hysteria. This is the opposite of the journey of Lear.

For the play to make sense—and to sustain the remorseless passage from absolute to zero—the Lear of the opening scene has to be a King with no visible chinks in his ironclad armour. But even if they are not visible, the chinks are there. The gradual self-discovery of his vast ignorance is the motor of the action. It is the richness of this discovery that gradually seeps and then floods through the gaps.

Shakespeare always shows how in every powerful character there are layers of unsuspected weaknesses. This leads us into tragedy—what has been called the 'hidden flaw'. But what gives the pure element to tragedy and separates it from melodrama is that a tragic hero—from Oedipus on—is a valid human being.

Today, we have many psychological and neurological terms which show the same embarrassing truth—none of us is born as a white sheet. Even astrological charts, with their complex diagrams of the influences at work at the moment of birth, are saying the same thing. The Greeks called it 'destiny'; the word today is 'genetic'. Shakespeare explored many ways in which a human being is born with inbuilt limits and how in some cases he or she can go beyond them. This is a theme that Shakespeare pursued from *Coriolanus* through *Measure for Measure* to *The Tempest*. Sophocles achieved this in *Oedipus* by placing his hero in front of a growing series of events through which the truth had to appear. In *Coriolanus* we find a deeply hidden sensitivity that becomes the source of tragedy when events compel it to emerge. Coriolanus, the warrior, is first presented in the verse with striking images based on iron—the structure of armour with which his every battle is won. Perhaps as a child it was his mother who conditioned him to believe that a patriotic hero was what life expected of him. This would be similar to the conditioning of empire-builders in Victorian British public schools. Volumnia constructed her son with Roman values.

Alas, deep down was a nature that not only contained pride, anger and violence—Coriolanus was someone else. A long series of trials and defeats was needed for his fundamental sensitivity to emerge. He seems uncompromising. He goes over to the enemy. His wish for vengeance and destruction, even on his own people, is a theme with which today we are painfully familiar. But Coriolanus has a mother who knows how far this is from her son's true nature, and, in one of the most magnificently conceived human situations, the mother is compelled to bring out all the qualities of her son to a late, but absolute fruition. As a Roman, she saves Rome and seals Coriolanus's doom. The inevitable tragedy is the destruction of a son through the insight of the one who had constructed his persona.

In *Measure for Measure*, Shakespeare has the two natures revealed by creating two separate individuals. The Duke has to descend from his eyrie to discover the life of the people. Angelo is a deputy who becomes a substitute despot and tries to imitate what he thinks is the autocrat's role by denying his subjects and himself the possibility of warmth, laughter and accepted sin. The pivotal moment is when Isabella suddenly and unexpectedly realises that mercy is greater than revenge.

If *King Lear* is the pinnacle of all European writings, matched only by *The Brothers Karamazov*, it is due to the total integration of every one of its parts into a whole, encompassing almost all of social, familial, political, personal and inner life. It is a blindness for actors to approach any one of the characters in *Lear* with prejudged stereotypes in mind. From the daughters to their husbands—one seeming weak, one ruthless—no simple adjective can encompass them. Brought to life from within—which is the actor's task—Kent, Gloucester, Edmund, Edgar, Cornwall, Albany are rich and dense.

In our *King Lear* with Paul Scofield in 1962, a magnificent actress, Irene Worth, made Goneril unforgettable by entering deeply into her uniquely from Goneril's own point of view. She showed a Goneril misunderstood and maltreated who always knew she was in the right. She made us sympathise with a daughter who has invited her father to stay and discovers the price she and her household have to pay. She sees a rabble of drunken knights ruining her home and humiliating the servants. Every daughter in the audience who has had a difficult father for a long stay will understand this at once. The more closely we follow her hurt feelings—going back no doubt to childhood—the greater the shock with which we witness the inexorable movement from sympathetic outer layers to a core that is harder and more violent than even her husband could have believed. Her ruthless, sex-fuelled nature is only revealed when Lear, in an extreme of cruelty, makes an appalling curse, calling for the destruction of any life that could ever arise in her womb. This is so appalling that for a moment we can almost accept and condone her driving her father out into the storm. We can understand its inevitability—the seed of tragedy has been born from the collision of two powerfully conditioned psyches.

So how was Shakespeare to exteriorise in *Lear* the fact that the impetuous, cruel tyrant of the first scene is a man of such buried quality that we need to follow more and more deeply his road to self-knowledge and compassion? He finds from the start a device—the Fool —whose voice is also Lear's inner voice which he refuses to hear and yet at the same time knows to be true.

There are two fundamental antitheses in *Lear* which reflect the universal human condition. They are blindness versus sight and the contrast between within and without. Both are shown as concrete realities and as limitless metaphors. Within the castle, protected by thick, impenetrable walls, life is warm and sheltered. In the psyche of the characters it is the same. The walls have to be broken, their comfort and protection totally removed, for the inner torments to be experienced. The citadel that some eighty years have built in Lear can only lose its defensive bastions one by one. It is the same with Gloucester until he and Lear are two equals, side by side. As he prepares to die, Gloucester finds a point of repose. He discovers that 'Ripeness is all'. Lear has to go much further.

It would be pointless here to try to explore all the intertwining threads of this work. They can only be rediscovered in rehearsals and above all in moments of truth in performance. I am not attempting here to describe Paul Scofield's all-encompassing playing of Lear. It had to be experienced to be known.

At first, in the storm, Lear is still strong enough to defy the elements. But Lear soon begins a new phase. Like the Duke in *Measure*, he leaves the palace, for the first time, to experience directly the life of his subjects and then of the human creature itself—a journey of revelation. But he is still protected by his memories and his personality. With uncanny precision Shakespeare proceeds as a psychologist, a neurologist and a sociologist. Lear's mind is totally unable to cope with this flood of new impressions. But the tsunami is irresistible. The last line of defence has to yield. The only refuge is the one he fears most—madness.

This is as far as many authors could go. But in Shakespeare's epic tale it is just the beginning of a new chapter.

The physically blind and the mentally blind old men, Gloucester and Lear, come together to exchange a new vision and understanding of the beings around them who have had to lie and flatter to reach their own ends. Only now is Lear ready with infinite pain and yet a new suggestion of calm, to recognise Cordelia, her true quality and his own blindness.

What follows next could easily be a happy end. Lear can accept all that comes his way as long as he is united in love with his daughter. But the tale is pitiless—a final barrier that has to fall if his essential truth is at last to appear. Cordelia must pay for her act of rebellion. Cordelia must die, she must lie there in her father's arms—and his last efforts to find sense and pattern fail. There are only these unforgettable words to take us to the heart of tragedy:

Never ... never ... never ... never ... never.

Many commentators have wondered why there is no note of Christianity to give the audience consolation in the end.

Of course, like all religions, the religion of Christ has of necessity outside walls and hidden inner meaning. The Father, the Throne, the Golden Gates of Paradise, the fires of Hell are at first necessary supports. But on the deepest level, reassuring imagery gives way to an infinite, vibrant and luminous void. This is where all Lear's tragic struggle has led him. But as in every play of Shakespeare's, tragedy never has the last word. Life on every level has to go on. Here it is for Edgar to bring a new opening:

We that are young
Shall never see so much, nor live so long.

Taken literally, this does not make any sense at all. It is not as though the story is all about the achievement of living to a ripe old age. This is a poet and a dramatist's expression of how much can be compacted into each unit of time—if we are aware enough to perceive it. For Lear it is the crowding of extreme pressures into the last period of his life that make every second of his final experiences another lifetime. And we, the spectators, have witnessed the intensity of existence that is crowded into each moment of the play. We too have 'seen so much'. Seeing is the result of suffering transcending blindness, and 'live so long' is where 'never, never, never, never . . .' leads. It is an opening to eternity.

The Hour Glass
Every Grain Helps

In the Middle Ages, a monk would keep a skull and an hour glass before him on his table. Each grain of sand that fell was a reminder of time—how short, how easily wasted, how each passing moment is gone for ever.

In this image we can see all the aspects of the difference between everyday time and theatre time, as much for the player, the director, the spectator as for the writer. 'Two hours' traffic' can be no more than a way of killing time—or else the concentration of experiences as in *King Lear* that otherwise could take a lifetime.

Everything suggests that Shakespeare wrote at great speed. It would seem that his quiet and gentle surface covered a pressure cooker of swirling and even explosive atoms of thought, feeling, memory and experience. For this reason, our starting point in approaching his verse is to recognise the concentration and density of each phrase, often deceptively simple and, within the phrase, each word, whose shape, duration and sound are all inseparable from its meaning. When I worked with Ted Hughes to develop a language of invented words for *Orghast*, he was fascinated to observe in himself the inner process of a poet. Gradually, he found he could capture the exact moment when a meaning began to search for a form.

In the nineteenth-century theatre, speeches were taken as slabs of resonance, and only the greatly talented actors by pure intuition could centre into the detailed life of words where thought and feeling unite.

In the twentieth century, as a reaction against bombast, a cool, scholarly approach arose. It taught a new generation of actors to study the structure of the verse as separable from its meaning. This led many actors to the same impasse as opera singers are brought to by their teachers. Shakespeare was often described as writing plays that were halfway to opera, and it is useful to see how dangerous this can be.

Clearly, in both cases, the only starting point is to feel what inspired the writer or composer to his first sounds or words. In almost every case there were human characters in a particular human situation. If the author or composer was touched by this, the rest followed.

But, in the world of opera, it begins differently. Here an artist first encounters a new role with a very precise and demanding teacher at the piano, who corrects him or her on the details of tempo and pitch, long before the living context, the situation itself, is even considered. Of course, they know the story roughly. It is the fine detail of each situation that is the guide. Words appear, and it is these words that gave the composer his melody. This seems so simple, but it is amazing how easy it is to overlook.

It can easily be the same with verse-speaking. Until recently, the Shakespearean actor had to be taught the rules of verse—the ten beats, the possible divisions into five plus five, the stops at the end of each line, and so on—before being brought into contact with the source of the writer's inspiration and even more the shape, pattern and rhythm of the thought itself. For true thought has a feeling, and it is the feeling that has a music in its flow.

Shakespeare, in the passionate velocity of finding words for the formless tumult within him, never counted from one to ten. This was a deep part of his consciousness, and so in his mature writing, when the pressure of the feeling was stronger than correctness, he violated his own rules.

When he wrote for *Lear*, 'Never ... never ... never ... never ... never ...', did he realise—and is it of any use for the actor to know—that these five words form a perfect pentameter? If the actor observed the beat, the result would be wooden and lifeless. When spoken by a great actor like Paul Scofield, the music was different at every single performance. It could not be otherwise. He was not thinking, 'How can I renew this bit tonight? How can I say it differently?' He had no choice. He reached this moment in the fifth act, with the whole intense succession of events alive in him. Then the words inevitably appeared with the only rhythms that came out of that evening's experience. So rehearsal, listening to the others, getting closer and closer to the partner, improvisation and then the presence of an audience are all tools for sharpening the actor's inbuilt sensitivity. This is method without method.

Many years ago, a simple experience brought into sharp relief the art of the poet in transforming everyday time into theatre time. Peter Weiss, the author of *Marat/Sade*, was a politically committed humanist, a painter mainly of collages and above all a poet. Deeply motivated by the horrors of the Holocaust, he felt the need to bring this into the immediate awareness of a theatre audience. So he plunged into transcripts of the Nuremberg Trials, lived them, suffered them and then distilled the hundreds of pages of direct spoken testimonials into a minimum of words, natural, intense and precise. In this way, he put at the service of truth all that a poet's skills could bring. The result was so powerful that the hour glass dominated the event. Each grain of sand that fell became a scorching flame.

Let us relate this to *Hamlet* for a moment and take a passage from 'To be or not to be':

> *Thus conscience does make cowards of us all*
> *And thus the native hue of resolution*
> *Is sicklied oe'r with the pale cast of thought*
> *And enterprises of great pith and moment*
> *With this regard their currents turn awry*
> *And lose the name of action.*

' ... Is sicklied o'er with the pale cast of thought ...!' 'Sicklied ... pale cast ... thought': the series is magnificent. But we can easily imagine a teacher sending back an essay to a pupil saying '"sicklied over" is an unattractive use of words, do better next time!'

The more we allow ourselves to enter deeply into the inner life of the character, the more we can recognise the rightness of 'sicklied'. In *Hamlet*, the talented young prince is not only examining all that he has so far accepted in court life, but is now putting in doubt his own education and his natural ease with speech. 'Words, words, words . . .' are a deep questioning—what is their true value? In this context we see that the hard shock of 'sicklied' leads straight to a new discovery: thoughts which seemed so inseparably part of all search for truth are suddenly seen as no more than pallid imprints. Of course, the whole speech and its questioning has to be there to illuminate this moment, but it is enough for now to look back to the preceding line.

Thus conscience does make cowards of us all

Introspection, awareness are contained in 'conscience', which intuitively enabled Shakespeare to give a vivid strength to self-examination by the use of a harder sound in 'cowards', and with the undoubtedly immediate and intuitive presence of the percussive sound, by using the cacophony of a repeated 'c'. Can it help actors to know this, even if they have taken a university degree? Or is it, rather, not a developed sensibility to every aspect of a line, its shape, its sound and its meaning that can give the preparation needed?

The hour glass is present in the lines that follow. We can see how they are the compression of what otherwise—outside of theatre time—could call for so many words, words and even more words. The words are no longer separate details; they are part of one powerful phrase which leads to a conclusion that touches on the whole painful journey Hamlet has to make.

> *And enterprises of great pith and moment*
> *With this regard their currents turn awry*

There are many ways of approaching

> *enterprises of great pith and moment*

Someone following the theoretical rules could be led into making three stresses:

> *enterprises—of great pith—and moment*

Another, trying to make everything natural and modern—'This is how I'd say it'—could add a fourth stress:

enterprises of great pith and moment

Or even a fifth:

enterprises of great pith and moment

In different ways, each version is missing the power of a line which, taken as a whole, expresses vividly one single thought. It is not necessary to give importance to a word by a stress. The word can be filled with a special meaning without breaking the flow of the lines.

enterprisesofgreatpithandmoment …

This does not need to be gabbled, nor broken up. Its life comes from changing vocal colours. These are not 'stressed'—the colours arise naturally from thought and feeling without losing the shape of the phrase. The movement continues—

… with this regard their currents turn awry

—to reach a conclusion of simple clarity with six light everyday words:

And lose the name of action.

So the one even simpler word, 'action', carries the weight of all that has prepared us for its appearance and its place in Hamlet's life at that moment.

The musical equivalent is finding a freedom from the metronome. Peter Hall called this 'free jazz'. The beat is there as a constant reminder of the hour glass. Free jazz is never sloppy. The beat is there but is no tyrant. The phrase takes its own shape, surfing the waves.

Verse speakers and opera singers could learn a great deal if they listen to all forms of popular music from Billie Holiday to Edith Piaf, where the passion, the feeling, the intonation, the tempo all arise from the word. In Broadway jargon, this is called 'reading' a song. I once asked Richard Rodgers, composer of *Oklahoma!* and countless other musicals, whether he had a stash of melodies in a top drawer, waiting to be used. 'Of course not!' he said. 'I need the words.' Like every composer of songs, it is the words that are proposed by a lyric that awaken the tune.

In Georgian traditional music, the word used is 'saying'—'saying a song'. The beat is there but the phrase has a purpose.

When the hour glass is present, each falling speck of sand reminds us how, in this special form called 'theatre', great enterprises can so easily lose the name of 'action'. The grain of sand tells us that 'meaning' cannot be described, it cannot be analysed. But when its truth is present, it is part of the action. Within each grain, which at first sight is one single speck, there are infinite shades of detail that can be revealed. Between two grains of sand, there is a moment of suspension. We are touched, and intimately we say 'Yes'. The hour glass is not clockwork; it is not a voice shouting, 'Hurry up!' It is a reminder that a life is always just so long, but each moment is unpredictable, never twice the same. In Shakespeare the words are like tiny sperms, each with its own direction, its own purpose. We try to put ourselves at its disposal, and this calls for all we can bring: patience, impatience, hurry, calm. The grains seem identical, but this is an illusion. The life in between is always on the move.

This leads to a thrilling mystery. In terms of style and structure, verse is at the opposite pole to everyday speech. In normal relationships we do not talk to one another in verse or song. This dichotomy can lead in totally opposite directions. It can produce a stage idiom that the cultivated spectator accepts as artificial. The lines and the characters are killed instantly if we try to reconstruct the period in which they were written, as though Shakespeare was just a product of his times. In fact, productions from all over the world constantly give us new views of the plays. The exceptional African actor Sotigui Kouyaté, in *The Tempest*, brought to Prospero a culture where the invisible was a constant part of nature, of his own daily experience. It was the same for Bakary Sangaré as Ariel. This Ariel had the powerful body of a footballer, not the lithe dancer we so often see. But the lightness came from within. He knew the spirit and we saw it with him. Wondrously, when the thought and feeling are perfectly blended, the most unusual phrase, sound or gesture becomes perfectly natural. This must always be the test. When at the moment of experience it seems natural, the question does not even arise. We are touched in a new way—there is no time for anything else. Just meaning. That's what verse is all about.

A Cook and a Concept

Dreaming the *Dream*

Once a computer was asked, 'What is the truth?' It took a very long time before the reply came, 'I will tell you a story ...'

Today, this is the only way I can answer the question I've been asked so often: 'Why don't you write about *A Midsummer Night's Dream*? You must have so much to say!'

So—I'll tell you a story.

When I was eighteen or nineteen, my one ambition was to make a film. By chance, I met the most eminent producer of the day, Sir Alexander Korda, a Hungarian of humble origins who had emigrated to make his fortune first in France, then in Britain, where he rose to power, was ennobled by the King and married a beautiful star, Merle Oberon, who for my father was 'the perfect woman'.

I had just been on a trip to Seville during Holy Week, was thrilled by the multitude of mysterious impressions and imagined a story set in this extraordinary background.

'Sir Alexander,' I began, 'I have an idea for a film—'

He cut me off with an unforgettable phrase that contained in a few words the period in which it was uttered, the British class system and the snobbery of a newly enlisted member of the upper classes. With a light dismissal of the hand he said: 'Even a cook can have an idea.'

This was virtually the end of the meeting. 'Come back when you have developed your "idea" enough to have a real story to offer me.'

It took many years to free his phrase from its period and context and to hear the deep truth it contained.

This brings me directly to *A Midsummer Night's Dream*. It had never occurred to me to think of directing the *Dream*. I had seen many charming productions with pretty scenery and enthusiastic girls pretending to be fairies. Yet, when I was invited to do the play in Stratford, I discovered to my surprise that my answer was 'Yes'. Somewhere in me there was an intuition that I had ignored.

Then, the first visit to Europe of the Peking Circus revealed that in the lightness and speed of anonymous bodies performing astonishing acrobatics without exhibitionism, it was pure spirit that appeared. This was a pointer to go beyond illustration to evocation, and I began to imagine a co-production with the Chinese. A year later, in New York, it was a ballet of Jerome Robbins that opened another door. A small group of dancers around a piano brought into fresh and magical life the same Chopin nocturnes that had always been inseparable from the trappings of tutus, painted trees and moonlight. In timeless clothes, they just danced. These pointers encouraged a burning hunch that, somewhere, an unexpected form was waiting to be discovered.

I talked this over with Trevor Nunn, director of the Royal Shakespeare Theatre, who said for this season he had created a young company who could in no time learn anything that was needed. It seemed too good to be true, especially as the Chinese Circus acrobats started their training at the age of five.

So we began with only the conviction that if we worked long, hard and joyfully on all the aspects of the play, a form would gradually appear. We started preparing the ground to give this form a chance. Within each day we improvised the characters and the story, practised acrobatics and then passing from the body to the mind, discussed and analysed the text line by line, with no idea of where this was leading us. There was no chaos, only a firm guide, the sense of an unknown form calling us to continue.

Through freedom and joy, Alan Howard as Oberon not only found very quickly that he could master the art of spinning a plate on a pointed stick but that he could do so on a trapeze without losing any of the fine nuances of his exceptionally sensitive verse-speaking. His Puck, John Kane, did the same, while mastering walking on stilts. In another register, a very talented and tragically short-lived young actor, Glynne Lewis, discovered that all the accepted ideas of Thisbe's lament over Pyramus's death being a moment of pure farce were covering a true depth of feeling. This suddenly turned the usually preposterous attempts at acting of the 'mechanicals' in the palace into something true and even moving. The situation was reversed and the smart and superior sniggering of the cultivated spectators well deserved the Duke's rebuke:

For never anything can be amiss
When simpleness and duty tender it.

Then, for the first time, we used a practice that we can no longer do without. In the middle of rehearsals, we invited a group of kids into our rehearsal room; then later we asked an *ad hoc* crowd in a Birmingham social club, so as to test what we were doing. Immediately, strengths and lamentable weakness were pitilessly exposed. We saw the trap of rehearsal jokes—everything that made the company fall about with laughter fell flat. It was clear that some embryonic forms could be developed and others discarded, although in the process nothing was lost. One thing can always lead to another. On French level crossings there is an apt warning: 'One train can conceal another.' This can have a hopeful reading: 'Behind a bad idea a good one can be waiting to appear.'

Gradually, the jigsaw began to fit, yet the very first preview was a disaster. My old friend Peter Hall took me by the arm and expressed his regret at the bad flop that was on its way. But at this point in the process a shock was needed. What to do? Peter Hall's close collaborator John Barton said, 'The problem is at the start. The way you begin doesn't prepare us for the unexpected approach that follows. As it is now, we just can't get into it.' Thanks to John, we found a way of starting the play literally with a bang. With an explosion of percussion from the composer Richard Peaslee, the whole cast literally burst onto the stage, climbed up the ladders and swarmed across the top level of the set with such joy and energy that they swept the audience along with them. After this, they could do no wrong. The presence of the audience in a week of previews and a high-pressured re-examination of every detail allowed at last the latent form to appear. Then, like the well-cooked meal, there was nothing to fiddle with, just to taste and enjoy. Often, after an opening, one has to go on working day after day, never satisfied, but this time we could recognise it. Miraculously it had fallen into place.

When the production had played across the world, there were many proposals to film it. I always refused because the essence of designer Sally Jacobs's imagery was a white box. The invisible, the forest, even the darkness of night were evoked by the imagination in the nothingness that had no statement to make and needed no illustration. Unfortunately, the cinema of the day depended entirely on celluloid, and after the first screenings more and more scratches would appear. In any event, photography is essentially naturalistic and a film based only on whiteness, least of all a soiled and blotchy one, was unthinkable. Of course, a play can be filmed, but not literally. I've attempted this many times, and always a new form had to be found to correspond with a new medium. It can never be a literal recording of what the audience in the theatre once saw. Here I felt that nothing could reflect the zest and invention of the whole group. This truly was a live event.

Then the production was invited to Japan. Everyone was eager to go. As the costs were so high, could I agree to it being tele-recorded in performance so that it could be shown all over Japan and so contribute to their expenses? If we all agreed, they promised the recording would be destroyed in the presence of the British Consul. I discussed this with the cast, who had all been with me in refusing filming. This time it seemed impossible for us to say 'No'.

A few weeks later, I received a bulky parcel from Japan. It contained a set of large discs. 'This,' wrote one of the producers, 'is a copy of the recording. We feel that you should have it.'

I found a player and discovered to my amazement that it looked very good. I sent a cable to Japan, telling them not to destroy the master. At once a telegram returned. 'This morning, in the presence of the British Consul, as you requested, the recording and the negative have been burned.'

Only later did I realise that this was a valuable reminder to stay with my own convictions. The life of a play begins and ends in the moment of performance. This is where author, actors and directors express all they have to say. If the event has a future, this can only lie in the memories of those who were present and who retained a trace in their hearts. This is the only place for our *Dream*. No form nor interpretation is for ever. A form has to become fixed for a short time, then it has to go. As the world changes, there will and must be new and totally unpredictable *Dreams*.

Today, more than ever, I am left with a respect for the formless hunch which was our guide, and it has left me with a profound suspicion of the now much-used word 'concept'. Of course, even a cook has a concept, but it becomes real during the cooking, and a meal is not made to last. Unfortunately, in the visual arts, 'concept' now replaces all the qualities of hard-earned skills of execution and development. In their place, ideas are developed as ideas, as theoretical statements that lead to equally intellectual statements and discussions in their place. The loss is not in words but in the draining away of what only comes from direct experience, which can challenge the mind and feeling by the quality it brings.

A used carpet placed over a mass of old, used shoes won international prizes. It was considered enough to express the tragedy of emigrations, of displaced people and their long march. This made an admirable piece of political correctness, but its impact was negligible when compared with Goya, Picasso or many shockingly intense photographs. A single light bulb going on and off won an important award because it expressed all of life and death. In fact, it only expressed the 'idea' of life and death. These have been prize-winning concepts, but would not Alexander Korda rightly have said, 'Come back when you have put your idea into a powerful form'?

A form exists on every visible and invisible level. Through the quality of its development, then in the way its meaning is transformed. It is an understandable difficulty for actors, directors and designers facing a play of Shakespeare not to ask, 'What should we do with it?' So much has been done already and so often filmed, recorded or described that it is hard not to begin by searching for something striking and new. A young director's future may depend on the impact he or she makes. It is hard to have to play characters like Rosencrantz and Guildenstern without looking desperately for an idea. This is the trap opening under the feet of every director. Any scene in Shakespeare can be vulgarised almost out of recognition with the wish to have a modern concept. This easily leads to spicing the words by having a drunk say them into a mobile phone or else peppering the text with obscene expletives. This is no exaggeration. I saw the videotape of an actor trying vainly to find a new way of saying 'To be or not to be'. As a last resort, one evening he set out to see whether alcohol might not be the answer. So he set up a camera, put a bottle of whisky on a table beside him, also a clock, and at planned intervals during the night recorded himself doing the soliloquy again and again as he gradually poured the contents of the bottle down his throat. The result needs no comment. Fortunately, there is another way. Always, an ever-finer form is waiting to be found through patient and sensitive trial and error. Directors are asked, 'What is your concept?' The critics write about 'a new concept' as though this label could cover the process. A concept is the result and comes at the end. Every form is possible if it is discovered by probing deeper and deeper into the story, into the words and into the human beings that we call the characters. If the concept is imposed in advance by a dominating mind, it closes all the doors.

We can all have an idea, but what can give the dish its substance and its taste?

There Is a World Elsewhere
The Readiness Is All

My father loved quotations. This line from *Coriolanus*—'There is a world elsewhere'—was one of his favourites, and he would quote it again and again. I grew up knowing that it encompassed more than a bitter warrior's rejection of his native city. It is not only the slamming of a door. It is an instinctive recognition that there are always other doors that are opening.

I have my own list, and the lines that for me stay closest are Lear's 'I have taken too little care of this', Hamlet's 'The readiness is all', and Gloucester's 'I see it feelingly'. The words are so simple. Perhaps the most astonishing example of this is six words that have found their way across the world. Al Pacino made the experiment, crossing a busy street in New York to ask the most unlikely passer-by, 'What do you know about Shakespeare?' The answer was immediate:

'To be or not to be.' But why? How can we understand this?

The question lies in something we take for granted as though it were sliced bread—the 'word'. Is this a pellet, is this a crumb?

The hour glass gives us one aspect of time—each grain that drops is lost for ever. But time has many dimensions and in the end, time opens to timelessness.

So in a single word, even in the word 'word', there are all levels that the Elizabethan playhouse reflects— from the marketplace to the transcendental. How does this fit with the conviction that Shakespeare wrote at the speed of his thought?

John Gielgud was the finest verse speaker of his generation. He never theorised. His deep sense of meaning was instantaneous. The physical act of speaking at once called into being all that his thought and feeling could offer. So much so that he was a unique neurological phenomenon. The movement of his tongue was an inseparable part of the movement of his thought. This led him into well-known and much-loved gaffes. Some terrible comment on an actor's work would arise in his mind and at once the thought was spoken out loud. This would be followed by a lightning-speed, truly felt apology: 'Sorry, dear boy, I didn't mean you.' Later in life, as a middle-aged actor, he was encouraged to play for the last time a Hamlet that had been a revelation when he was young. Although I loved him dearly, I was surprised and disappointed. Over the years, he had answered so many questions, had heard so many interpretations of every line, that his playing was slow and was completely blocked by the pale cast of thought. It was a lecture, not a performance, as though he read out all footnotes as he spoke. I had a similar experience when I staged *Hamlet* for the first time. Full of awe and respect for this great challenge, I closely studied all the detailed analyses I could lay my hands on. As a result, intuition had no place, and the production was dull, except for Paul Scofield, who refused all discussion and analyses. He went his own way, and when we played in Moscow, the audiences, so accustomed to elderly Hamlets' laboured interpretations in ponderously long productions, were completely bowled over by the clarity and speed. This could help us to discriminate between the self-conscious writer enriching his phrases with well-chosen words—and the immediate phrase, where thought and meaning arise together. For this reason the line is not literary but so simple that it becomes a normal act of speaking. Like:

The readiness is all.

Inside the readiness is the rich residue of experience. Consciously guarded, or unconsciously buried, it is a link to the collective unconscious. When actors can call the word to resonate in them, this residue of experience can rise up into awareness.

'Readiness.' The word is unusual; it's not one we use in everyday conversation. And yet at the moment we say or hear it, it seems completely right. There is once again no sense of an author carefully making literature. The rightness is all.

In this triad of ever-so-simple phrases, we can find as many levels of life as Shakespeare's tumultuous times must have brought into them.

A word is like a glove—an inanimate object to be admired in a shop window or even in a museum. But life is given by the hand that fills it—every shade from banal to expressive.

When I first worked at Stratford, actors were expected to bring diction, resonance, volume. If they did so, they were told that the words will speak for themselves. In my first production of a Shakespeare play—*King John* at the Birmingham Rep—I described the core of old stalwart actors as 'The Booming Barons'. It was much later that the notion arose that actors should seek out the character reality and human truth already contained in Shakespeare's words, waiting for the thinking, feeling hand to enter the glove.

A word can be more than a glove. It is a magnet. When it is poised over an inner empty space, as it is spoken it can bring to the surface material buried in the unconscious. And in very special moments, it can draw on the shared material of humanity.

When we look at a printed page of Beckett's plays, we see almost every short line followed by 'Pause'. This was Beckett's Advice to the Players. Chekhov did the same, but for 'Pause' he used ' . . . '. For the simple series of words to take on the fullest human dimension, the speaker must trust the resonances that arise in these tiny gaps. These moments of silence exist in films, in prose. But in theatre, in the recreation together with the audience of a phrase at each performance, the pause, the three dots can never be the same. It is the hallmark of life's presence.

Many years later, when we were already installed in the Mobilier National in Paris doing our first period of research, a young Englishwoman came to see me. She was very troubled. As was the vogue in the sixties, she had joined an experimental group. It was run by a fairly successful conventional director who had been swept away by the startling new ideas of the Living Theatre and Grotowski. Abandoning all his West End experience, he turned to new ways that he had picked up by hearsay. He brought with him the authority of his reputation. His group was highly disciplined and readily accepted him as its leader and guide. She, too, had done so faithfully for months and now was sadly disillusioned. 'I've come to realise that there was nothing in his ideas. They were only words, beautiful words.'

This opened the door: words, the same words, the same phrases, can so easily deceive us. If they are beautiful we are seduced and forget that the same words, like the glove, can be full or empty.

Stanislavsky never began with theories; he only formulated them after a long career of searching. Yet students believe that they can start from the conclusion—what was put into words becomes a recipe or a road map, and how often they find it takes them nowhere. I take great care when a young director asks me to pass on what I have learned. Each time, I'm haunted by the English actress: 'Only words, only beautiful words.'

The Quality of Mercy
On Prospero

Among Shakespeare's best-known words are 'Quality of mercy', but before approaching those words 'quality' and 'mercy', I would like to come back again to *Love's Labour's Lost*. This play, by a young man full of all the images which come from feeling that life in every one of its forms, is an extraordinary, amazing and intoxicating experience. When I first saw this play—and then, very soon afterwards, was in the happy position of staging it—I was struck by something which seemed to me so obvious. At the end of this extraordinary, seemingly artificial, dancing comedy, just before the very end, before the moment when of course everything has to be happily reconciled, suddenly—and you could almost say without any apparent necessity—death comes into the story.

A group of people who have been living a joyful life in a golden world suddenly are made to recognise that the golden world is a part, and not the whole, of existence. Why, we can ask, did Shakespeare in this play go beyond the conventions, not only of his time, but of all comedy writers, and make so poignantly intense this very last moment? I didn't give an answer—it only seemed to me that the quality of the experience that the audience lived in this play would be transformed and heightened if this moment were given the value that the author intended. If this play suddenly introduced an enigmatic coexistence of light and dark, it seemed to me that this was the impression that Shakespeare wished the audience to carry away, because it corresponded to something in his own experience.

We look at the rest of Shakespeare's plays, at the whole extraordinary range of characters, situations and experiences, at the astonishing richness of the outside world, the social world, the political world, the psychological world and the spiritual world that go through all the plays. Then we reach Shakespeare's last play, *The Tempest*. Ask any Shakespeare lovers if they can remember the last word of Shakespeare's last play. As far as we can tell, this could well be the last creative word that he wrote. The last word of *The Tempest* is 'free'.

It is interesting to think that the whole movement of Shakespeare's search for understanding could have led him to ending his last play with a character—Prospero himself—saying to the audience, 'Set me free.' So, what precedes these words? Prospero has just said, 'My ending is despair.' This too could be the end; why not? There are many plays, many contemporary plays, many plays in the twentieth century, many, many plays right through our time, whose authors would consider this an excellent way of ending the evening: 'My ending is despair.' Either 'Curtain' at one period or 'Blackout' at another. And the audience, after a short moment, would applaud vigorously because it would understand and sympathise with what the author is trying to say. But in fact as Shakespeare wrote this he had something further that he felt it essential to say—for the phrase continues with a qualification: 'Unless it be relieved by prayer.' If we take a naive, Sunday-school reading of these words, we are in something horrendously banal because, were Shakespeare to have made this his ending, he would have got out of the misery-trap of ending on despair, by putting in its place a vague, pious and totally degraded word, 'prayer', on whose meaning no two people can agree. Instead Shakespeare says stop, listen: prayer must be understood for what it really is. I am not talking about a prayer, he says, which is just

'Please give me this or that, please do this for me'; Prospero is saying that he needs a prayer which 'pierces so that it assaults mercy itself'. Where is the Zen master who has given to his pupils such an enigma? Is there a Koan more challenging than each element in this phrase?

'A prayer which pierces' is already something that one can spend many years in a monastery trying to understand. What is a piercing prayer, that pierces so that it assaults? How can a prayer assault, and what is it assaulting? It assaults Mercy. Shakespeare firmly places together the words 'mercy' and 'assault' and out of that clear yet obscure, incomprehensible paradox that stops the mind comes a very simple resolution, which is that crimes—very strong word—are pardoned and that through indulgence freedom can arise. If I go into the detail of this it's also because one of the greatest dangers, I think, that all of us who practise the staging of Shakespeare encounter is the tendency to simplify and reduce. Very often the last speech of Prospero is taken to be a charming, elegant, conventional winding-up of a play. It's even said that Prospero here is no longer Prospero but the actor himself coming forward at the curtain call and saying, 'Dear friends, the play is now over; we thank the designer, we thank the musician, would you please be kind enough to give us your hands for applause and then we can all go home.' Everyone who has seen the play many times has heard these words presented as a conventional curtain speech. There are many books of criticism which say this is simply the actor's winding-up in the conventions of the comic theatre, that the play is a romantic comedy which is charmingly brought to a close by this little rhyming speech. On the other hand, if one just looks at what is written, one sees that such an attitude is totally impossible: no actor who is following what is written can say 'My ending is despair unless it be relieved by prayer which assaults mercy', as though these were unimportant words.

There are countless themes in Shakespeare, but constantly his writing is dominated by the question of order and chaos, chaos and order—what is chaos, what is the place of chaos, what is order, what do we mean by order, what can order bring, what is its relation to chaos? These are perhaps the themes that are closest to our lives, both externally and within, at this moment of history. We are within chaos—we can't deny it, and the chaos around us is an inner chaos—everyone recognises this, I think, very simply, in themselves. There is a profound, and sometimes despairing, need for order. And yet we are at a moment when we perhaps rightly see that we can't follow the apparent meaning of either. For chaos cannot only be equated with an absolute disaster. Chaos is more than something totally catastrophic; chaos and catastrophe are not exactly the same. And order, we see, is constantly betrayed; every prophet, every leader who has stood up in public to try to call us towards an order, has always betrayed order by placing some invented, even beautifully invented order in its place. We long for order, and yet we are beginning today to be more respectful of chaos. We can feel the tremendous and dynamic power of forces when they are set free. And we can love and respect the extraordinary quality of stillness that even a candle can express, of how the chaos of fire is not in contradiction with the understanding of the flame. This is the theme that runs through the whole of Shakespeare.

For instance, there are the comfortable, warm interiors of *King Lear*, where an old man has with magnificent, admirable and astonishing power and authority maintained an order, while outside there is the extraordinary force of nature, and the power of madness. The separation must be bridged. In *King Lear*, two completely different visions of human life, their meaning and their necessity, are presented in juxtaposition, in opposition and eventually in reconciliation. How? What reconciles them? In so many of the other plays, plays of war, plays of strife, plays of conflict, plays of antagonism, of hatred, of murder, of jealousy, one sees the notion of order, the notion of structure, challenged and swept away by tremendous energies. Without wishing to reduce Shakespeare to any one theme, this particular issue runs through play after play: great opposing sources of energy leading to dynamic conflicts. When one comes to *The Tempest* one sees this particular battle very clearly dramatised by Shakespeare within his final story.

Before the beginning of the play Prospero was a very fine, cultivated, sensitive, intelligent Duke. But he was a Duke who was thrown out, he was chucked out of his job, he was booted out of his palace, ruthlessly. And the interesting thing there is that one can't say 'poor man', or 'poor Milan', one can only say he deserved it. Why? Prospero deserved it because as a man sitting in libraries reading about spiritual issues, studying the occult, he was an admirable, romantic, somewhat dreamy individual—and clearly a very poor Duke. He had no notion of what is demanded of somebody in that position. In *Measure for Measure*, the Duke makes a first attempt to face this.

The Mahabharata arose from a need: to educate a young man at a moment in Indian history when to become a King was regarded as the greatest of roles. And the eighteen volumes of *The Mahabharata* are written uniquely to prepare a young man for the passage from naivety to understanding—understanding, that is, on every level: from understanding on the toughest practical level of how to use spies, to the understanding that comes to him through Krishna, and eventually to his deepest and most secret inner understanding of the nature of the living process itself.

The Mahabharata is there as a training document. Unfortunately, Prospero in all his reading didn't come across the volumes of *The Mahabharata*, so he sat there in romantic dreams, and his kingdom was not in order. His ruthless brother was a man who understood order in the crudest way, in the way that is always understood by politicians. Today there isn't a politician who doesn't at one time or other drag out of his vocabulary 'the necessity for order'. It's there within his party machine, within its whole structure. He gets himself elected by exploiting a tiny part of the great concept of order. And of course in the process he pulls the great concept down to something not only petty but ultimately dangerous and destructive.

So Prospero betrayed order, and his orderly brother came and restored his idea of order, got rid of Prospero, and Prospero was sent off in a rotting boat and found himself on a barren island. Prospero is shaken out of his comfortable Milanese dream, and he begins to face reality in a new way. Prospero is often reduced to a silly old man on an island. One can't imagine anything more extraordinary for a daughter than suddenly to be told the whole mystery of her past by her father, but I've actually seen this great scene done with the daughter yawning and showing to the audience, 'Oh, he's going on too much, I wish he'd just stop telling me all these boring old things about the past.'

However, if one looks at what is actually there in the play, one sees something very different and far more fascinating. Prospero is jolted out of his dream in a very harsh and difficult context, on an apparently barren island, and he has to learn about another world, he has to learn about the spirit world which he thought he could read about in books. Now he has to discover this in a tough way through his own experience. He encounters witches, spirits and, in Caliban, very violent forces.

What do we know about Prospero for sure—what isn't simply speculation? If you listen to his famous speech where he actually tells about his magic, he is very clear. He learned not just to be a magician who could do a few tricks and make food appear so that he and his daughter wouldn't starve, it wasn't just to have a few elves and goblins around as slaves, to serve at table and clean up his hut; he says very precisely that not only did he play joyful games with his spirits, but that he went further: he learned how to make thunder and lightning come into being at his command. In other words, he entered into a very dangerous game of power; he began to have power over the most basic energies and forces of Nature. And furthermore he says that he used this for his own entertainment, to open tombs and get corpses to arise. This is often glossed over, but very specifically it is what Prospero tells as being his own life. He has entered the chaos of natural forces, he has seen how a man can dominate them, command them and become a form of superman, and how that superman is then in a position to have revenge. He has reached an alarming pinnacle of human development; he has become a magician. He has power; he can take his revenge on his brother, who took away his dukedom; he can draw him into his hands.

Just at this point it's possible to put the question, 'Does that mean that he has become a free man? Is this freedom?' When I was seventeen, I read in a book on Magic that if you follow the incantations given you can call up armed men and beautiful women at your command. When I read this at the age of seventeen I thought, 'This is freedom.' What more can one ask of life than to sit with a book, to chant phrases and suddenly to have not only all the women that you want but also armed men to defend you from jealous lovers and husbands? This seemed the very image of a free man! And certainly Shakespeare very cunningly creates this trap for the audience, because he leads you to have a sneaking admiration for this super figure called a magician. But in *The Tempest* this isn't the end of the play, nor is it what the play is about. In the subplot, ambition, anger and revenge dominate. Trinculo, Stephano and Caliban conspire to murder Prospero. But Prospero recognises that he must abandon this magic completely, he must drown his books and break his wand. Only when he's done that is he able to take a totally new step, and this step is the step from vengeance to forgiveness. Now, at last, he's in a position of being a man like any other man. And now he can see that he cannot take on himself the pretension of judging his brother. All that he can do is to restore the island to Caliban, who is like a beginner in existence with his own path to follow, and then return to his old life. Although Prospero nominally becomes Duke again, he now knows his real need is to return to where he started, to *his* Milan, to his place of origin, to his source as a man amongst others, as a simple person.

This is still not where the play ends. He'll now go back, he says, and live a simple life and 'Every third thought shall be my grave'. Let's remember for a moment that sudden entry of death that gave meaning to *Love's Labour's Lost*; once again here every third thought is a thought of dying. But were Shakespeare to have made this his conclusion and not written the epilogue, something would be lacking, something still would be soft, hazy, vague, incomplete. This is where the play is, I think, a great challenge to our understanding. There is order and there is chaos. There is power and the abandoning of power. There is pride, and there is humility ... And yet in all these oppositions something is unspoken, is deeply lacking. What can encompass and bind them together? The opposition evokes a powerful question: out of the opposition, which in itself can go on for ever (because an opposition is dynamic and cannot graduate beyond its own level), what is lacking so that this constant dynamic opposition, on which all life as we know it is based, can be transformed? What is the element of transformation that is still not yet present in a

Prospero who has drowned his books, broken his wand, become humble, come back to ordinariness not as a dreamer now but as a man who has touched all the structures and fibres of life, and through this recognises that he is a man like another man? What is still lacking? And I think it is in order to touch this incomprehensible offer to mankind that's contained in the word 'free', that Shakespeare proposes 'a prayer which assaults mercy'. The thought is not new, for already he had brought into a previous play the conviction that there is a certain quality which none of us can see, none of us can define, and yet which has this total capacity of bringing about a true freedom—which he named 'the quality of mercy'. I would like to end with these two words. Quality and Mercy. The moment that one tries to pinpoint with one's ordinary argumentative understanding, one takes a step away from the possibility of another understanding. Quality, mercy, free: this trinity is the Shakespearean riddle.

Epilogue

This book began with the question, 'Who wrote Shakespeare?' The question is out of date. Whatever the label, it is the quality of the living experience that concerns us today. Nothing else.

For this, we have to recognise the millions of forms that tumbled out of this treasure chest called Shakespeare.

'Form'—and 'Quality'—are words whose simplicity is their downfall. These vast portmanteau terms contain an infinite series of levels leading from the ridiculous to the sublime and down again.

For every actor, director, collaborator, for every critic, there is only one treacherous, elusive and magnificent guide when one approaches these works. The guide cannot just be subjective, nor truly objective. A sliding scale means just that. We must continually look within at what is awakened when what is within meets what comes from without. What is the process through which the sense of a buried something gradually becomes a form? At the same time we must bring all we can to help this something to become what we are forced to call 'Quality'.

Shakespeare. Quality. Form. This is where our work begins. It can never end.

A Chronology of Peter Brook's Shakespeare Productions

1945 *King John*
      Birmingham Repertory Theatre

1946 *Love's Labour's Lost*
      Stratford-upon-Avon

1947 *Romeo and Juliet*
      Stratford-upon-Avon

1950 *Measure for Measure*
      Stratford-upon-Avon

1951 *The Winter's Tale*
      Phoenix Theatre, London

1955 *Titus Andronicus*
      Stratford-upon-Avon and European tour

      Hamlet
      Phoenix Theatre, London;
      Moscow Art Theatre, Moscow

1957   *The Tempest*
       Stratford-upon-Avon

1962   *King Lear*
       Stratford-upon-Avon;
       London; New York

1968   *The Tempest*
       Stratford-upon-Avon;
       Aldwych Theatre, London

1970   *A Midsummer Night's Dream*
       Stratford-upon-Avon

1972   *A Midsummer Night's Dream*
       New York and world tour

1974   *Timon of Athens*
       Bouffes du Nord, Paris

1978   *Measure for Measure*
       Bouffes du Nord, Paris

       Antony and Cleopatra
       Stratford-upon-Avon

1990   *The Tempest*
       Bouffes du Nord, Paris

2000   *The Tragedy of Hamlet* (in English)
        Bouffes du Nord, Paris

2002   *La Tragédie d'Hamlet* (in French)
        Bouffes du Nord, Paris

Index
of Play Titles and Characters

Aaron 36
Albany 57–8
Angelo 45–6, 49, 57
Antonio 103–4
Antony 49
Antony and Cleopatra 48–9, 112
Ariel 73
Armado 31

Bottom, Nick 10

Caliban 103, 105
Claudio 47
Cleopatra 48–9
Cordelia 54, 61
Coriolanus 56–7, 87
Coriolanus 56–7, 87
Cornwall 57–8

Desdemona 48

Edgar 57–8, 62
Edmund 57–8

Florizel 31
Flute, Francis 78
Fool 52, 59

Gloucester 57–61, 87
Goneril 53, 57–9
Gravedigger 17
Guildenstern 84

Hamlet 10, 16–17, 67–72, 84, 87–90
Hamlet 10, 16–17, 42, 67–72, 84, 87–90, 111, 113
Henry IV, Part Two 35
Hermione 31–2

Iago 48
Isabella 31, 45–8, 57

Juliet 19–21

Kent 57–8
King John 90–1, 111
King Lear 49, 51–62, 66, 87, 100–1
King Lear 10, 32, 49, 51–62, 63, 66, 87, 100–1, 112

Lady Macbeth 42
Lavinia 34–5, 38, 41
Leontes 31–2

Love's Labour's Lost   19, 29–31,
    95–6, 106, 111

Macbeth   42
Macbeth   42–3
Marcade   30–1, 95–6, 106
Measure for Measure   26, 31,
    45–9, 56–7, 60, 101, 111, 112
Merchant of Venice, The   95, 107
Mercutio   20, 23
Midsummer Night's Dream, A
    10–11, 75–85, 112
Miranda   103–4

Nurse, The   20–1

Oberon   78
Othello   36, 48–9
Othello   36, 48–9

Perdita   31
Polixenes   31
Princess of France   30
Prospero   49, 73, 95–107
Puck   78

Quince, Peter   10

Regan   53, 57–8
Richard III   35
Richard III   35, 42
Romeo   19–21, 23
Romeo and Juliet   19–27, 32, 46,
    63, 111
Rosencrantz   84

Shallow   35
Sonnets, The   13–14, 16–17
Stephano   105

Tamora   36, 38
Tempest, The   49, 56, 73, 95–107,
    112
Theseus   78–9
Timon   32–3
Timon of Athens   32–3, 112
Titus Andronicus   34–5, 38
Titus Andronicus   29–43, 54, 111
Trinculo   105
Twelfth Night   31

Vincentio   45–9, 57, 60, 101
Volumnia   56–7

Winter's Tale, The   31–2, 111